This Book Belongs to:

_____

*For bird lovers everywhere,
especially Evie and Lizzie:
strong-spirited and full of joy*

I See a Bird!

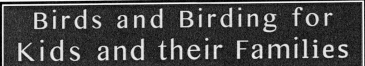

Birds and Birding for Kids and their Families

Written and Illustrated by
Jan Johnson Doerfer

LOONART DESIGNS

Traverse City, Michigan

Many thanks to John, Trish, Gail, Jacey,
& Jenny
and to The Cornell Lab of Ornithology

Published by Loonart Designs, Traverse City, Michigan, 49686
ISBN 978-0-692-68283-8
            0-692-68283-X

http://jdoerfer.wix.com/iseeabird

Contents

Sit softly on the ground--
sit quietly, don't make a sound.
Close your eyes. What do you hear?
Listen...birds are everywhere.

Many birds live in your backyard or in a park, forest, or lake near your home. You can watch birds anytime, anywhere, alone or with your family and friends. Best of all, birding doesn't have to cost a thing.

Use this book to help identify the birds you see and keep track of them on the following page. The poem under each bird's picture will give you clues to help you identify that bird.

At the end of the book you will find a list of resources to help you and your family learn more about birds, including websites you can use to listen to their songs.

Are you ready to have some fun?

Let's go birding!

My Bird List

Date	Bird	Location, Number, Info

AMERICAN CROW

Crow struts his stuff,
he is quite social,
CAW-CAW-CAW!
and very vocal!

SIZE: 17"- 21"

HABITAT: Woodlands, farms, and cities

RANGE: Throughout North America, sometimes gathering in roosts of thousands of birds

SIMILAR SPECIES: Fish Crow, Blackbird, Raven

BEST SEEN: In parks and neighborhoods as well as fields and woodlands; very social, they are usually seen in family groups, eating garbage left in picnic areas, or on roadsides or beaches

Crows are smart, inquisitive, and full of mischief. They are good learners, and have been taught to mimic the human voice. Crows eat just about any kind of food (including dog food left in your yard for your dog!) You will seldom see crows alone. They are family oriented, and young crows often stay with the family group for several years and help the parent birds raise new broods. Male and female crows look alike.

AMERICAN GOLDFINCH

They love thistle seeds,
what a treat!
Makes goldfinches sing:
"to-eat, to-eat, to-eat..."

SIZE: 4 ½"-5"
HABITAT: Thickets, grasslands, and open country; at bird feeders, especially those stocked with thistle seeds
RANGE: Throughout most of the U.S. and southeastern Canada
SIMILAR SPECIES: Pine Siskin, Yellow Warbler, Lesser Goldfinch
BEST SEEN: At feeders and perched on the stalks of seed- bearing plants

Goldfinches eat seeds and buds, and so they nest in midsummer when seeds are plentiful. The males are brilliant yellow, black, and white in spring and summer, but turn a buff olive color in winter. Females and young birds are dull colored in summer as well as winter. Goldfinches are flocking birds, and are often seen in the company of other kinds of finches. They are the state bird of Iowa, New Jersey, and Washington.

AMERICAN ROBIN

She eats one worm
and then another.
Robin Redbreast
sings for her supper.

SIZE: 9"-11"
HABITAT: Yards and gardens, parks, open woodlands and pastures
RANGE: Throughout North America; migrates in spring and autumn
SIMILAR SPECIES: Towhee, Orchard Oriole, Wood Thrush
BEST SEEN: Hopping across lawns, searching for, and tugging up, worms

Robins are an early sign of spring, though some robins stay in their territory throughout the winter. In the spring they might build their nest in the eaves around your house. Males and females look alike, but young robins have spotted breasts which later change to rusty red. Robins love a meal of earthworms, but they also eat many berries. If you need an alarm clock, the robin's cheerful morning song will wake you up. Robins are the state bird of Wisconsin, Michigan and Connecticut.

BALD EAGLE

I see an eagle soaring high,
her wings spread wide to meet the sky.
She quickly dives to catch a fish.
Her eaglets have a tasty dish.

SIZE: 28"-38"
HABITAT: Forests near open water
RANGE: Throughout North America
SIMILAR SPECIES: Osprey, Golden Eagle, Turkey Vulture, Red-Tailed Hawk
BEST SEEN: Soaring with a wide, **flat** wingspan near rivers and large bodies of water; look for their huge nests, most 4-5 ft. in diameter, located in the tops of trees

Bald Eagles are the national bird of the United States and are sacred to Native Americans. In the mid-1950s their numbers dropped to less than 500 breeding pairs due to pesticides which made their eggshells thin and brittle. After DDT was outlawed and eagles were placed on the Endangered Species List, their numbers soared. They are avid fishers and can dive up to 99 mph to catch a fish. They also rely upon other predators for food, often chasing them away from their kill and robbing them of dinner. Males and females look alike--dark brown with a white head and tail--but female adults are larger. Juveniles are mottled brown and white.

BLACK-CAPPED CHICKADEE

I see a bird
high in a tree.
He wears a black cap.
"Chick-a-dee-dee-dee...!"

SIZE: 4 ¾"- 5 ¾"
HABITAT: Forests, open woodlands, gardens, and parks
RANGE: Entire U.S.; remains throughout the year
SIMILAR CHICKADEE SPECIES: Boreal, Carolina, and Mountain Chickadees
BEST SEEN: At bird feeders, where their favorite seeds are sunflower and thistle, and flitting through branches in wooded areas

Chickadees are friendly, inquisitive little birds, often the first to visit a new bird feeder. With patience, they can be coaxed into eating sunflower seeds out of your hand! They are "grab and go" eaters, picking out a seed, and flying to a perch to eat it. Males and females look alike. Listen carefully and you'll hear them call out their name: "*chick-a-dee-dee-dee*," and their clear-noted song: "*feee-beeee*"; or could it be, "*feed*-me?"

BLUE JAY

Jay buries acorns in the ground
and often makes a noisy sound.
Big and bossy, bright blue crest,
he wears a "necktie" on his chest.

SIZE: 10"-12"
HABITAT: Oak forests, city gardens and parks
RANGE: East of the Rocky Mountains.; some migrate, some remain throughout the year
SIMILAR JAY SPECIES: In the west, Scrub Jay, Steller's Jay, and Pinyon Jay
BEST SEEN: Listen for their noisy, sometimes raucous calls. They prefer platform or tray feeders and will eat peanuts, sunflower seeds, and suet. Their bright blue coloring and large size make them easy to spot.

Blue Jays are handsome, intelligent, and social birds that learn by observing. They carry nuts and acorns in their mouths and throats and bury them in the ground to save for later, so we can thank them for planting thousands of oak trees. They also feed on insects, grains, and fruit. You can tell a Blue Jay is around when you hear loud squawks and a musical "wheedle-wheedle." Male and female Jays look alike.

CEDAR WAXWING

I see a flock of Waxwings
flitting through the trees,
feasting on our berries,
eating all they please!

SIZE: 5½"-7"
HABITAT: Mixed forests and fields, especially
along streams; orchards and gardens
SIMILAR SPECIES: Bohemian Waxwing
RANGE: Throughout North America
BEST SEEN: In flocks, frequently in fruiting trees
and bushes; attract them to your yard by planting
hawthorne, crabapple, winterberry, raspberry,
and other small fruiting bushes and trees

Cedar Waxwings are sleek, crested, flocking birds that eat mostly fruit, and some insects in the summer. They may appear suddenly to feed on ripe berries and then move on. The name "Waxwing" comes from the red waxy tips on their secondary wing feathers. Males and females look alike. They nest in late summer when fruit is plentiful. If you see a small flock of handsome masked birds, and hear a chorus of high pitched "zeeee"s, you'd better guard your berries!

COMMON LOON

Red eyes, black head,
checkered back--
she dives underwater
for a fishy snack!

SIZE: 28"-36"
HABITAT: Forested lakes and rivers in summer; coastal waters in winter
RANGE: Northern U.S., Alaska and Canada in summer; southern coasts in winter
SIMILAR LOON SPECIES: Red-throated, Pacific, and Arctic
BEST HEARD & SEEN: On northern lakes; listen for their ghostly calls

Loons are excellent underwater swimmers. They dive quickly-- now you see them, now you don't-- and swim long distances in search of fish. Loons need undisturbed wild shoreline to nest because their heavy bodies make it difficult to walk on land. In the water, baby chicks often hitch a ride on the backs of their parents. Male and female adults look alike, while chicks are soft, grayish brown. They have three unique calls: the wail, yodel, and tremolo which sounds like crazy laughing but is really a signal of distress. If you hear the tremolo, look at the sky. Do you see an eagle?

DARK-EYED JUNCO

Hopping, scratching on the ground,
Juncos make a trilling sound.
Bright white feathers line their tail.
Will they build a nest inside your pail?

SIZE: 5"-6 ½"
HABITAT: Mixed forests, parks, and backyard feeders
RANGE: Across U.S. and Canada in summer; winters into mid- and southern states
BEST SEEN: Watch for their white breast flashing and white stripes on sides of tail in flight; often seen beneath bird feeders, scratching for seeds

Juncos are one of the most common birds of North America and can be found from Alaska to Mexico, and California to New York. Males and females look alike, though there are regional differences in coloring from slate gray to buff brown. They are ground foragers so you will often see them under a feeder looking for seeds. They nest on slopes, sometimes in the roots of an upturned tree, but you may also be surprised to find a pair nesting in one of your garden pots.

DOWNY WOODPECKER

Tapping, tapping
like a drum,
I hear a woodpecker,
rum-a-tum-tum.

SIZE: 5 ½"- 6"
HABITAT: Woodlands, gardens, and parks
RANGE: Throughout U.S. and Canada
SIMILAR WOODPECKER SPECIES: Hairy, Ladder-backed, Northern three-toed, Yellow-bellied Sapsucker
BEST SEEN: Frequent visitors to bird feeders, they especially like suet. You might see them climbing a tree upside down.

Downy Woodpeckers are small birds with a bright black and white pattern on their wings and a spot of red on the back of the male's head. The female looks like the male without the red spot. They cling to trees and slender weeds, and hang from feeders, balancing like nimble acrobats. Listen for their high-pitched *"pic"* or shrill, whinnying call. Drumming on trees doesn't mean they are "pecking" for food, though they love to eat insects that live in tree bark. It's really a form of communication. Don't confuse them with the larger Hairy Woodpecker.

EASTERN BLUEBIRD

Bluebird, Bluebird!
He has no time to rest.
He's looking for a birdhouse,
where he can build a nest.

SIZE: 6 ½"- 8 ½"
HABITAT: Pastures and meadows
RANGE AND SPECIES: **Eastern Bluebird** (East of Rocky Mountains): blue with orange breast and throat; **Mountain Bluebird**: (Rocky Mountains): sky blue with blue to white belly; **Western Bluebird**: (Great Plains): blue with blue throat and buff breast
BEST SEEN: In open fields perched on fences and posts, and on top of nest boxes

B luebirds are a favorite sight in spring and summer. Males are bright blue in the sun, while the females are dull gray with hints of blue in their wings and tails. They nest in tree cavities created by woodpeckers (a good reason to leave dead trees standing), and in nest boxes which can be easily constructed and placed along the edge of fields. They eat berries and insects, and are often seen flying to the ground to snatch a bug.

GREAT HORNED OWL

Owl sits in a pine tree,
perched outside our house.
"Hooooo, hoo-hoo, hooo."
Owl spies a little mouse.

SIZE: 18"-25"
HABITAT: Forests, open country, and city parks
RANGE: Throughout North America
SIMILAR OWL SPECIES: Long-eared and Barred
BEST HEARD: At night, a series of far-carrying hoots: *HOO, hoo-HOOO, hoo, hoo*

Great Horned Owls live everywhere, from city parks to deep forests. Males and females look alike, but females are larger than males. Because they are nocturnal, they are difficult to see, but at dusk you may see a large, dark swooping owl, wings outspread, hunting for rabbits, mice, snakes, insects, or frogs. Their talons are strong enough to catch prey larger than themselves. For a clue to where they live and what they eat, look for owl "pellets"-- wads of undigested hair and bones that the owl has spit out--near the base of a tree. Their intense yellow eyes do not move, but the owl's head swivels 180 degrees.

HOUSE WREN

In the spring-soaked meadow
a happy wren trills.
Her bright song echoes
far across the hills.

SIZE: 4½"-5¼"
HABITAT: City parks, yards, farms and woodland edges
RANGE: Throughout U.S. and Southern Canada
SIMILAR WREN SPECIES: Canyon, Cactus, Bewick's, Winter, Carolina, and Marsh
BEST SEEN: In thickets, fields, and yards; listen for their exuberant song or harsh chatter, and look for their flicking upright tail

Wrens are energetic, eager little birds, and enthusiastic singers. They are cavity nesters and prefer nest boxes or dead trees in which to raise their young. They may even build a nest in an old boot, pail, or clothing left hanging in the yard. They eat a variety of insects and caterpillars, making them a welcome visitor to the garden. If you hear a wren making a harsh chatter or rattling call, it is most likely scolding a predator, probably a cat!

MOURNING DOVE

"Coo, coo-coo, coooo," cries the dove,
perched in a treetop, high above.
She fluffs her feathers, tucks her head.
The sun is setting. Time for bed.

SIZE: 9"-13"
HABITAT: Open woods, gardens, and parks
RANGE: Throughout U.S. and Canada
SIMILAR SPECIES: Rock Pigeon, Inca Dove, White-winged Dove
BEST SEEN: Often seen in pairs on open ground looking for seeds, or perched on a wire softly cooing; they feed at platform feeders or on the ground

Mourning Doves, like all birds, fluff their feathers to trap air between them. This provides insulation and holds in body heat like a down comforter. Doves look for food on the ground near brush and thickets where they can easily escape from predators. If you have bird feeders, make sure they are full when the sun is setting, as many birds feed at dusk to give them enough energy to keep warm during the night.

NORTHERN CARDINAL

The world is light.
The snow falls, white.
The Cardinal glows
in plumage bright.

SIZE: 8"-9"
HABITAT: Woodland edges, thickets, and gardens
RANGE: Atlantic coast to Great Plains, Midwest into Canada where they remain throughout winter
BEST SEEN: At bird feeders; pairs are usually seen together

Cardinals are a favorite bird of many people and the state bird of Illinois, Ohio, Indiana, Kentucky, North Carolina, Virginia, and West Virginia. The female cardinal is one of the few female songbirds that sings, maybe as a way of telling the male what food to bring to the nest. Cardinals have many beautiful songs, including "cheer-cheer-cheer" and "birdie-birdie-birdie." The male defends his territory, often chasing other birds from the feeder. They do not migrate and stand out vividly against the snow. Males are brilliant red, while females and young cardinals are soft grayish brown with red shadings.

RED-TAILED HAWK

Hawk perched on high--
a rabbit dashes.
Hawk soars and swoops.
Her red tail flashes.

SIZE: 18"-23"
HABITAT: Forests and open country
RANGE: Throughout North America
SIMILAR SPECIES: Red-shouldered Hawk, Swainson's Hawk
BEST SEEN: Perched on roadside trees or soaring over open country

Red-tailed Hawks are often seen high in the sky, circling over fields in search of small mammals and rodents. Watch roadside trees and wires for this large bird as it waits for movement in the brush below. You may hear them call in flight, a high-pitched, raspy *"screeee"* or *"keeeer"*. Hawks build large nests of sticks and branches in the crowns of trees or on cliff edges. From below, you can identify a Red-tailed Hawk by their rusty red tail feathers. Males and females look alike, but there are many variations in color from very dark to almost white.

RED-WINGED BLACKBIRD

In the marsh the blackbird sings.
Red and yellow mark his wings.
"Chonk-la-reee!" you'll hear him say.
The sun is warm and bright today.

SIZE: 7"- 9 ½"
HABITAT: Marshes, wetlands, and meadows
RANGE: Throughout the U.S. and Canada
SIMILAR SPECIES: Starling, Cowbird, Grackle
BEST SEEN: Usually seen and heard near water
or wetlands, perched on cattails and sedges

Red-winged Blackbirds are one of the first signs of spring in the north where the males sing their hearts out during breeding season. The males and females are distinctly different: males sport bright red and yellow shoulder patches which they can puff up, (when they want to "show off") or hide, (when they feel insecure.) Females are a dull, streaky brown. They gather in large flocks to roost or migrate. While Red-winged Blackbirds favor life near the water, you might see them in your backyard feasting on seeds that have dropped from your bird feeder since they are ground feeders.

RUBY-THROATED HUMMINGBIRD

Hummingbird hovers.
Hummingbird sips.
Hummingbird buzzes.
Hummingbird zzzzzzzips!

SIZE: 3½"
HABITAT: Woodlands, gardens, parks
RANGE: Eastern U.S. and Canada
SIMILAR HUMMINGBIRD SPECIES: Rufous, Anna's, and Broad-tailed
BEST SEEN: Sipping nectar from garden flowers, and feeders filled with plain sugar water (4 parts water:1 part sugar--do not add dye!)

Hummingbirds are active eaters, attracted to tubular flowers like bee balm and petunias, and feeders filled with fresh sugar water. Their tiny nests (only 2 inches wide!) are woven of spider silk and lichens, with dandelion, cattail, or thistle down lining the inside. They usually lay two eggs, each one the size of a pearl. They are the only birds that fly backward and hover like a helicopter. During courtship, the male does a ritual pendulum dance, flying in a wide arc and buzzing loudly, showing off his bright red throat.

SANDHILL CRANE

When spring grows warm,
the cranes fly north.
When cold winds blow,
it's south they go!

SIZE: 34"- 48"
HABITAT: Marshes, ponds, & wetlands
RANGE: Mexico to Southern U.S. in winter, Central and Northern U.S. to Canada in summer
SIMILAR SPECIES: Whooping Crane, Great Blue Heron
BEST SEEN: Mid-March & early October through the plains, Wisconsin and Michigan; often viewed in large flocks in grain fields, pastures, and wetlands

Cranes migrate in large flocks in spring and fall, sometimes numbering in the thousands. They fly in a loose "V", necks and legs outstretched, often very high in the sky. You may hear them before you see them, as they have a distinctive rolling, "croaking" call in flight. They feed on grains in farm fields, and frogs and small fish, making them sensitive to pesticides and herbicides. During courtship, Cranes are graceful and skilled dancers, stretching their wings, bowing, and leaping into the air.

SONG SPARROW

Sweet, sweet, sweet--
I hear the sparrow's song.
She's singing in our cherry tree
all day long.

- SIZE: 5"-7"
  HABITAT: Thickets, pastures, gardens and parks with open habitat
- RANGE: Throughout North America
  SIMILAR SPARROW SPECIES: Fox, Swamp, Lincoln's, Vesper, and White-throated
- BEST SEEN: On the ground and in low vegetation under trees and shrubs

Song Sparrows are common visitors to bird feeders, though they feed mostly on spilled seed on the ground. They also eat a variety of insects and fruits. Males and females look alike with streaking on their chests and flanks, and sometimes a dark spot on their breast. Their song begins with three identical notes followed by a trilled note and series of short notes sung from a high perch on twig or shrub. They flick their tails up and down in flight, a telltale sign of these cheerful birds. If you see a bird singing with great enthusiasm, it's probably the Song Sparrow.

WHITE-BREASTED NUTHATCH

Nuthatch climbs trees upside down...

Nuthatches are often seen at feeders in the company of Titmice. Watch them creep down tree trunks in search of insects. Titmice build nests in holes and cavities of dead trees. They line their nests with hair, sometimes plucked from live animals or even people! Listen for "Peter, Peter, Peter."

TUFTED TITMOUSE

..and Titmouse wears a pointed crown.

SIZE: 5"-6"
HABITAT: Mixed forests
RANGE: Nuthatch: throughout North
America; Titmouse: Eastern U.S. and
variations in the Southwest and California
BEST SEEN: In mixed forests; they are
frequent visitors to bird feeders

Resources/Websites

WEBSITES WITH INFORMATION ABOUT BIRDS:

- **CORNELL LAB OF ORNITHOLOGY:** Cornell University
  www.allaboutbirds.org/
  > Bird identification including photos, video,
  > bird calls, how to attract birds, bird webcams,
  > Living Bird Magazine and ebird
  >
  > > Listen to bird calls

- **NATIONAL AUDUBON SOCIETY**
  www.audubon.org/
  > Bird guides with links to bird songs and calls,
  > conservation information, Audubon Magazine
  >
  > > Listen to bird calls

- **AMERICAN BIRD CONSERVANCY**
  www.abcbirds.org/
  > Information and news related to the
  > conservation of birds and their habitat

- **AMERICAN BIRDING ASSOCIATION**
  www.aba.org/
  > Focused on recreational birding with a link for
  > young birders

Helping Birds

10 THINGS YOU CAN DO TO HELP BIRDS

. Participate in **The Christmas Bird Count** at **audubon.org** and/or **The Great Backyard Bird Count** at **gbbc.birdcount.org.**

. Put up nesting boxes, feeders, and bird baths. See how you can build your own: **http://nestwatch.org/learn all-about-birdhouses/**

. Plant bird-friendly shrubs, trees, native flowers and grasses in your yard.

. Avoid using pesticides and chemicals.

. Don't cut down trees, even dead ones, unless they're dangerous; provide brush piles and natural areas around your house.

Don't leave fish line in the water. It can get wrapped around birds causing them to die.

Keep cats away from birds.

Clean up after yourself and others by picking up litter and discarding your trash.

Stay on trails, don't trample vegetation, and avoid areas where birds are nesting.

). Share what you learn about birds with your family and friends.

Scientific Names of Birds

You don't need to know the scientific names of birds to enjoy birding, but it's a world-wide way to identify birds and bird families, no matter what language you speak.

American Crow	*Corvus brachyrhynchos*
American Goldfinch	*Carduelis tristis*
American Robin	*Turdis migratorius*
Bald Eagle	*Haliaeetus leucocephalus*
Black-capped Chickadee	*Parus atricapillus*
Blue Jay	*Cyanocitta cristata*
Cedar Waxwing	*Bombycilla cedrorum*
Common Loon	*Gavia immer*
Dark-eyed Junco	*Junco hyemalis*
Downy Woodpecker	*Picoides pubescens*
Eastern Bluebird	*Sialia sialis*
Great Horned Owl	*Bubo virginianus*
House Wren	*Troglodytes aedon*
Mourning Dove	*Zenaida macroura*
Northern Cardinal	*Cardinalis cardinalis*
Red-tailed Hawk	*Buteo jamaicensis*
Red-winged Blackbird	*Agelaius phoeniceus*
Ruby-throated Hummingbird	*Archilochus colubris*
Sandhill Crane	*Grus canadensis*
Song Sparrow	*Melospiza melodia*
Tufted Titmouse	*Parus bicolor*
White-breasted Nuthatch	*Sitta carolinensis*

Birding Essentials

Be ready to go birding by keeping a small pack or bag you can stock with the following items:

- comfortable shoes or boots that are okay to get wet and/or muddy

- binoculars, if you have them

- rain jacket, sweatshirt, and windbreaker

- mosquito repellent

- sunscreen and sunglasses

- water bottle

- sandwich or snacks

- hat with a brim (and gloves in case it's cold)

- notebook and pencil to keep track of the birds you see

- small bag for litter

- long pants to prevent scratches and poison ivy

WHEN YOU GO BIRDING BE PREPARED FOR CHANGING WEATHER AND ALWAYS BE ESPECIALLY CAREFUL NEAR WATER.

Made in the USA
San Bernardino, CA
24 August 2018